DATE DUE

DEMCO 38-297

ACKNOWLEDGEMENTS

Excerpts from the following sources appear in this volume:

George Anderson, "Group Praying in Jail," in *Review for Religious,* January 1978. Reprinted by permission.

Continued on page 125

PHOTO CREDITS

Orville Andrews/FPG 110
R. Burke/CORN'S 100
Ed Buryn/JEROBOAM 44
Jack Corn/CORN'S 28
George Daniel/PHOTO RESEARCHERS 92
Milan Dvorak/FPG 24
Editorial Photocolor Archives 54
Freelance Photographers Guild 2
Keith Gunnar/TOM STACK 104
Eric Hobbs/CORN'S 32
Peter Karas/FPG 62
William Koechling 118
Jean-Claude LeJeune 78, 88, 96
Roger Lubin/JEROBOAM 74
Jaimie Montemayor 20, 36, 40, 58, 114
Photo Researchers 12
H. Armstrong Roberts 8
Strix Pix 70
Samuel Uretsky/EPA 16
Edward Wallowitch 82
Jim Whitmer 50, 66

FIRST EDITION

Printed in the United States of America.

ARGUS COMMUNICATIONS
A Division of DLM, Inc.
One DLM Park
Allen, Texas 75002 U.S.A.

International Standard Book Number: 0-89505-050-1
Library of Congress Number: 80-67553

0 9 8 7 6

DECISION

"Jesus said,
'Let us go off . . .
to some place where we will be alone. . . .'
So they started out in a boat by themselves
to a lonely place."

MARK 6:31–32

1

Breakaway Invitation

Many people wake up each morning
not to the sound of an alarm clock, but
to the whir of a vibrator under their pillows.
These people live in a silent world.
They are deaf.

Most of us
think that blindness is worse than deafness.
But Helen Keller, who was blind and deaf,
considered deafness the greater handicap.

When you are without hearing,
an important door to the everyday world closes.
Turning on the radio is useless.
Watching TV becomes a bland experience.
You can't understand the people around you,
even their simplest questions.
You begin to feel lonely and abandoned.

Soon, you begin avoiding the hearing world,
associating only with the deaf.
You become a stranger in your own land.

The tragic plight of the deaf
illustrates the plight of many Christians today.
They have become strangers in their own land.
Spiritually, they have become deaf and dumb—
unable to speak to God in prayer,
and unable to hear God speak to them.

Though this spiritual plight is as old as time,
it is especially prevalent in modern times.
Tennessee Williams refers to it in his play
The Night of the Iguana:

Hannah: Liquor isn't your problem,
          Mr. Shannon.

Shannon: What is my problem, Miss Jelkes?

Hannah: The oldest one in the world—
          the need to believe
          in something or in someone.

What can we do about this problem?
Laurence Gould answers bluntly:
"We must stop gagging on the world 'spiritual'.
We must rediscover and reassert our faith."

But how do we refind and reassert our faith?
The gospel points to the answer.

One day, some people brought
a deaf and dumb man to Jesus to be healed.
Jesus took the man off alone,
away from the crowd, and restored his health.

To be healed
of our spiritual deafness and dumbness
we must present ourselves to Jesus for healing.
Concretely, this means we must "break away"
from the crowd, go off with Jesus alone,
and spend time with him in daily prayer.

4

Reflection

There is only one way
to understand the gospel fully—on our knees.
In other words, we must
pass beyond gospel study to gospel prayer.
We must cease being gospel spectators
and become gospel participants.

Imagine you are the man in this story.
Experience with all your senses
everything the man sees, feels, and hears.

"Some people brought [Jesus] a man
who was deaf and could hardly speak,
and they begged Jesus
to place his hands on him.

"So Jesus took him off alone,
away from the crowd,
put his fingers in the man's ears,
spat, and touched the man's tongue.
Then Jesus looked up to heaven,
gave a deep groan, and said to the man,
'Ephphatha,' which means, 'Open up!'

"At once the man was able to hear,
and his speech impediment was removed,
and he began to talk without any trouble. . . .
All who heard were completely amazed.
'How well he does everything!' they exclaimed.
'He even causes the deaf to hear
and the dumb to speak!'"
MARK 7:32-37

2

Considering It

Richard Armstrong and Edward Watkin
tell the story of a biologist's experiment
with "processional caterpillars."
On the rim of a clay pot that held a plant,
he lined them up so that the leader
was head-to-tail with the last caterpillar.

The tiny creatures circled
the rim of the pot for a full week.
Not once did any one of them break away
to go over to the plant and eat.
Eventually, all caterpillars
died from exhaustion and starvation.

The story of the processional caterpillars
is a kind of parable of human behavior.
People are reluctant to break away
from the rhythmic pattern of daily life.
They don't want to be different.

We must break away, however,
if we are to accept Jesus' invitation
to "go off alone" with him in prayer.
We must break away and be different.

This is especially difficult in today's world.
J. D. Salinger points this out in "Teddy."

"I mean it's very hard to meditate
and live a spiritual life in America.

"People think you're a freak if you try to.
My father thinks I'm a freak, in a way.
And my mother—well,
she doesn't think it's good for me
to think about God all the time.
She thinks it's bad for my health."

The decision to begin a meditation program
is a deeper commitment than people realize.
A story will illustrate.
One day a boy was watching a holy man
praying on the banks of a river in India.
When the holy man completed his prayer,
the boy went over and asked him,
"Will you teach me to pray?"

The holy man studied the boy's face carefully.
Then he gripped the boy's head in his hands
and plunged it forcefully into the water.
The boy struggled frantically,
trying to free himself in order to breathe.
Finally, the holy man released his hold.

When the boy was able to get his breath,
he gasped, "What did you do that for?"
The holy man said:
"I just gave you your first lesson!"
"What do you mean?" asked the astonished boy.
"Well," said the holy man,
"when you long to pray
as much as you longed to breathe
when your head was underwater—only then
will I be able to teach you to pray."

"It's a special place here.
It is God's place,
and more beautiful than you'd ever dreamed.
It's a heaven here,
yes, a heaven, but in some mystical way,
different from the one you seek. . . .
You feel you are dreaming,
yet no dream was ever so real."
MIKE VALENTINO

Reflection

Tim stood in the open doorway of the plane.
A 90-mile-an-hour wind howled past.
He recalled the words of his instructor, Bill:
"Fall like a badminton bird:
body arched, belly pointed downward,
arms and legs upstretched like feathers."
Later, Tim described what happened:

"Stepping out onto the locked wheel,
I grabbed the strut, then hung there. . . .

"Bill shouted, 'Go!'
I let go of the strut and arched. . . .
I could see the plane overhead. . . .

"Then, suddenly, there was a jolt . . .
and I was brought upright. . . .
The sky was silent,
like the inside of a vast cathedral,
and I could hear the beating of my heart."

Deciding to embark on a meditation program
is a lot like deciding to sky dive.
The very thought of it is frightening.
Once you make the decision, however,
a whole new world opens up to you.

Jesus said, "'Let us go off . . .
to some place where we will be alone. . . .'
So they started out in a boat by themselves
to a lonely place."

MARK 6:31-32

3

Breaking Away

Edmund Burke was giving his famous speech
against Warren Hastings.
Suddenly, he stopped in the middle of it.
There he stood for a full ten seconds
with his finger pointed at Hastings.
Not a person in the packed audience moved.
Then Burke resumed.

Afterwards, an opponent said to Burke,
"That was the most effective pause
I have ever seen.
I was holding my own breath
wondering what you were going to say next."
Burke grinned. "That's what I was doing too."

A pause or break
improves not only our speaking performance
but our living performance as well.
Consider this example.

When a British ship
encounters an unexpected disaster at sea,
the "Still" is sounded. The signal means
"Pause! Check your situation!
Determine the wise thing to do."

When the Still first sounds,
few crew members know the wise thing to do.
But during the pause enforced by the signal,
they discover it.

Pausing to go off alone with Jesus in prayer
not only gives Jesus a chance to heal us
but gives us a chance to evaluate our lives.
We need to do this regularly.

Bandello, who lived at Santa Maria in Italy
when Leonardo da Vinci was painting
his famous "Last Supper" there, wrote:

"I watched Leonardo work from dawn to dusk
without putting down his brush.
Then he would pause
and not put his brush to the canvas for days,
but spend a few hours each day looking at it,
examining and evaluating its figures."

Living is a lot like painting.
We must pause now and then
to examine the picture
we are producing on the canvas of life.
Two final points about a meditation program.

First, don't expect too much from it initially.
Above all, don't expect special things to happen.
Meditation cannot be forced.
It will develop gradually in its own way.
Start with five minutes; lengthen the time later.

Second, the joy and fruit of meditation
often occurs *outside* the time of meditation.
That is, later on in the day
you will do something or see something
as you would never have done it or seen it
were you not a meditating person.

Breaking away for his first experience into backpacking, Mike Partit writes:

"I expect a miracle from the first steps, a sudden relief of worldly burdens. It never happens. . . . Perhaps it's like meditation, or tennis; ask too much of it and you lose it all, double-faulting in the wind."

Reflection

Imagine
your body relaxing and becoming very light.

Feel it floating weightlessly into the air.
Feel it going up or down at your wish.
You can command it to go anywhere—
down into the ocean to explore the sandy floor,
up into outer space to visit a beautiful star,
out across the sea to an island beach.

When you are ready, go wherever you wish.

Where are you? Why did you come here?
What do you see? What do you hear?
How do you feel—peaceful, relaxed, liberated?

What can you do in this place
that you can't do in normal, everyday life?
During the next few minutes, let yourself go
and do whatever strikes your wildest fancy.

"Lord . . .
You know everything I do;
from far away you understand all my thoughts. . . .
You know all my actions. . . .

"If I went up to heaven, you would be there. . . .
If I flew away beyond the east
or lived in the farthest place in the west,
you would be there to lead me,
you would be there to help me."

PSALM 139:1-10

4
Finding a Place

Shortly before game-time on a hot afternoon,
Bill Freehan, 11 times an All-Star catcher,
sat in the corner of an empty shower room.
He was doing what he does
to prepare for every game: concentrating.

Preparation for competition
is not too unlike preparation for meditation.
The first step is the one Bill Freehan took
to prepare for his game:
finding a place to be alone.
Jesus often did this.

*"The next morning, long before daylight,
Jesus got up and left the house.
He went out of town to a lonely place,
where he prayed."* Mark 1:35

The first requirement for a "prayer place"
is that it afford reasonable privacy.
But there are other considerations.

Take the Little Brothers, a religious order.
Their vocation is to live among the poor,
praying for them and sharing their lot.

The first thing a Little Brother does
when he moves into a poor area
is to set up a place where he can pray.

Often a mat is sufficient,
placed before a wall on which hangs a cross.

But not everyone can set aside a place
in a busy household.
Thus, New York social worker Dorothy Day
says she used to do her daily praying
"in the little Italian church
on Twelfth Street."
When business made this impossible,
she says she meditated "on the fly":

"Not in the privacy of a study—
but here, there, and everywhere—at the
kitchen table, on the train, on the ferry,
on the way to and from appointments."

Regardless of where you choose to meditate,
start your program with complete openness.
Don't begin it with any preconceptions.
An example may help.

Did you ever bite into something
thinking it was one thing, only to find
something completely different?
The taste shock so surprised you
that you almost spit it out.

Meditation is something like that.
Approach it with a preconceived expectancy
and it may disappoint you.
Approach it openly
and it will delight you, in time,
with its own taste and its own enjoyment.

"Step softly under snow or rain
To find the place where men can pray.
The place is all so very plain
That we may lose the way."
G. K. CHESTERTON

Reflection

"One night
I was sleeping out under the stars, all alone.
I was alone because my camping partners
thought a thunderstorm was coming up.
They decided to sleep in a shack nearby.

"In the middle of the night,
I awoke with a start.
The feeling of a storm was intensely in the air.
Lightning was flashing everywhere.
Strangely enough, I wasn't at all afraid,
because God's presence seemed everywhere.

"Then the sky went completely black
and it began to rain and to thunder.
I sat under a tree, spellbound,
marvelling at God's power in the storm."

HIGH SCHOOL STUDENT: ADAPTED

*"How great is God's power. . . .
It is God who takes water from the earth
and turns it into drops of rain.
He lets the rain pour from the clouds
in showers for all mankind. . . .*

*"He sends the lightning across the sky,
from one end of the earth to the other.
Then the roar of his voice is heard,
the majestic sound of thunder. . . .
At God's command amazing things happen. . . .
The glory of God fills us with awe."*

JOB 36:22-37:22

5

Picking a Time

Comedian Eddie Cantor was in a hurry
to "make it big."
"Don't hurry so much," his grandmother said,
"or you'll miss the scenery." He raced on.

One night the curtain came down on a big hit.
Excitement exploded backstage.
Just then, a telegram came from his wife.
Their fourth daughter had just been born.
His grandmother's words echoed in his ears.
Later, Cantor said: "Ever since that moment,
I've taken time to pause and enjoy the scenery."

When you ask people why they don't meditate,
they frequently say with some regret:
"I'd like to, but I can't seem to find the time."

We are all slaves to the face whose 12 numbers
are counted endlessly by two tireless hands.
And this can be said with reasonable certitude:
If we don't make a serious effort to schedule
prayer into our day, we probably won't pray.

Four "prayer times" are popular with people:
after rising, during the noon lunch break,
before supper, immediately before retiring.
Finding the right time takes experimentation,
because people respond to time differently.
An example may illustrate.

Plants housed in total darkness
retain a time cycle that corresponds roughly
to our 24-hour day-and-night cycle.
In other words, they keep accurate time
without the aid of light.

"Body clocks" are also found in people.
"Body time," however, differs from "clock time."
For children, it seems to move more slowly.
For adults, it seems to move more quickly.
The difference is traceable to "cell cycles."
Time seems to pass more slowly
for children, whose cells are very active.
Time seems to pass more quickly
for adults, whose cells are less active.

Some people maintain that a similar phenomenon
is present also in each day.
Morning time seems faster for some people;
afternoon or night time for others.

Some people maintain, also, they function better
in the morning than in the afternoon.
For example, a salesman checked and found
that he made most of his sales before noon.
He adjusted his schedule; sales climbed.

All this affects our choice of a prayer time.
A person who finds that he functions better
in the morning might be advised to pray then.
Finding the prayer time that fits you best
may take months, but it is worth the effort.
Prayer is that important.

"The wind is one of my sounds.
A lonely sound, perhaps, but soothing.
Everybody should have his personal sound
to listen for—
sounds that make him exhilarated and alive,
or quiet and calm."

ANDRE KOSTELANETZ

Reflection

"I was riding my bicycle along the river bank.
After a while I became tired
and stopped at an old beaver dam to rest.
Sitting there, all alone, I began to notice
how quiet and peaceful everything was—
only the sound of water spilling over the dam.
I closed my eyes, relaxed, and listened.

"After listening to the water for some time,
I asked myself
where all this peace and beauty came from.
I kept coming back to the thought
that God put it here for all to find and enjoy.

"I wondered why I hadn't noticed it before.
Then I realized that the peace and beauty
were always there.
I just hadn't taken the time to notice before."

TOM BISHOP: ADAPTED

"Praise the Lord, my soul!

"O Lord, my God, how great you are! . . .

You make springs flow in the valleys,
and rivers run between the hills.
They provide water for the wild animals. . . .
From the sky you send rain on the hills,
and the earth is filled with your blessings. . . .
Lord, you have made so many things!
How wisely you made them all! . . .

"Praise the Lord, my soul!"

PSALM 104

6

Choosing a Posture

"He folded his large brown hands
across his chest, uplifted closed eyes,
and offered a prayer so deeply devout
that he seemed kneeling and praying
at the bottom of the sea."
HERMAN MELVILLE

When we think of the body at prayer,
we think of kneeling and of folded hands.
The Bible mentions kneeling,
but this isn't the only biblical prayer posture.

Nowhere does the Bible mention
praying with folded hands.
Folding one's hands in prayer originated
with the shackling of prisoners' hands.
From this beginning, the gesture evolved
into a sign of total submission.
Christianity carried the gesture a step further,
making it a sign of one's submission to God—
especially during the time of prayer.

Besides helping us to pray better,
bodily posture frequently says something
about the sincerity of our prayers.
When we converse, say psychologists,
the minor element is our words.
Of greater importance is the body language
that accompanies our words.
To make this point, psychologists note

that even the words "I hate you"
can be made to sound appealing.
In other words, the body speaks in prayer
just as eloquently as does the tongue.

A popular body posture for prayer is sitting.
There are two styles:
1) sitting erect in a chair, feet on the floor,
   hands in the lap or on the chair arms;
2) sitting on the floor, cross-legged, with back
   straight (possibly pressed against a wall),
   hands in the lap or resting on the knees.

The latter posture combines rest with alertness.
It may take a few weeks to get used to,
but the time and the effort are well worth it.
If you find it painful at first, be encouraged
by Anthony de Mello's experience:

"During a buddhist retreat I made,
we were asked to sit
for a whole hour at a stretch without moving.
I happened to be sitting cross-legged
and the pain in my knees and back
became so intense it was excruciating. . . .
And I thought I should faint with pain—
until I decided not to fight it . . .
but to become aware of it, to identify with it.
I broke the pain sensation up into its component
parts and I discovered, to my surprise,
that it was composed of many sensations. . . .
For the first time in my life
I was experiencing pain without suffering."

"I was at the seashore, all alone,
when these thoughts flooded in on me. . . .
Something prompted me to kneel on the sand
before this immense ocean, symbol of the infinite.
I felt that I prayed that day
in a way that I never prayed before."

MALWIDA VON MEYSENBUG

Reflection

It is late in the afternoon of a hot day.
You are alone on a rocky ocean beach,
enjoying the pounding sea and the singing gulls.

All of a sudden the sky clouds over,
a breeze stirs, and drops of rain start to fall.
See the raindrops fall on the ocean water,
forming millions of little rings.
Listen to the rain fall—
on the rocks and on the sand around you.

Feel the rain fall on your body, soothing it,
running down your shoulders, arms, and face.
Taste the rain as it falls on your parched lips
and trickles across them.
Smell the freshness of the air.

Suddenly, a feeling of joy floods your soul.
You feel at peace with everything.
You just lie there on the beach in the rain
grateful that you are alive—
grateful that you are part
of the magnificent world God has created.

"O Lord, our Lord,
your greatness is seen in all the world! . . .
What is man, that you think of him;
mere man, that you care for him?
Yet you made him inferior only to yourself;
you have crowned him with glory and honor."

PSALM 8:1-5

7

Pausing to Relax

When told he handled notes beautifully,
a pianist responded:
"The notes I handle like all other pianists;
the beauty is in the pause between the notes."

The pause is important in meditation also.
A pause *before* meditation can spell
the difference between success and failure.
It keeps us from entering meditation routinely.

A pause also reminds us to relax our bodies.
Most of us "drive with the brake on."
We live and work under habitual tension.
The key to releasing the "brake"
is to relax the body's major tension zones.

One of these zones is the forehead.
Under stress we tend to wrinkle it,
which only makes our problems seem worse.
Relax the forehead and problems seem smaller.
Another zone is the jaw.
Under stress we tend to clench it,
warning our brains: "We've got a big problem!"
Relax the jaw and the warning is canceled.
A third zone is the chest.
Under stress it tightens, restricting breathing.
When the stress subsides, we sigh:
"That's off my chest; I can breathe again!"

Under stress we also tend to "chest breathe,"
which is the way we breathe in emergencies—
as when running a race, for example.
We need oxygen fast, so our chest heaves
as we gulp in great volumes of air.

Nervous people use chest breathing
even in non-emergency situations.
Non-emergency breathing is "belly breathing."
It is next to impossible
to feel tense when you belly breathe.

Finally, tension is related to hurry.
We can hurry while sitting down doing nothing.
What should we do when we become aware
of feeling hurried?
The answer is simple: slow down!

We all have our own internal, natural rhythm.
If we let "hurry" destroy that rhythm,
we temporarily lose control of ourselves.

"The great Finnish runner, Paavo Nurmi,
always carried a watch with him in his races.
He referred to it, not to the other runners.
He never hurried but insisted on running
his own race, keeping his own tempo,
regardless of competition. . . .

"Life is not a 100-yard dash,
but more in the nature of a cross-country run.
If we sprint all the time, we not only fail to
win the race but we may not last
long enough to reach the goal."
JOSEPH A. KENNEDY

"Sometimes when
I've had to work to the point of exhaustion,
. . . I drop everything
and take an hour or so to sit relaxed,
eyes closed, groping for self-awareness.
. . . After such impromptu meditation,
I usually return to work feeling refreshed,
even exhilarated."
JOHN KORD LAGEMANN

Reflection

The champion race car driver Jackie Stewart
used an unusual method
to relax himself before each race.

Sitting in his car, he closed his eyes and
imagined his body was an inflated beach ball.
He would then imagine the air escaping it,
and feel his body deflating into a slab of rubber
that snugly fit the shape of the car seat.
This exercise relaxed him
not only physically but mentally.

Imagine *your* body is an inflated beach ball.
Imagine the air beginning to escape slowly.
Feel yourself deflating gently—
until you reach a point of perfect comfort,
every part of your body totally relaxed.

Now imagine all mental activities slowing down
and gradually coming to a complete stop.
Feel all mental and physical tension float away.
Now just rest there, completely relaxed,
bathed in peace and comfort.

Jesus said: *"Come to me, all of you
who are tired from carrying heavy loads,
and I will give you rest. . . .
Learn from me,
because I am gentle and humble in spirit. . . .
The yoke I will give you is easy,
and the load I will put on you is light."*
MATTHEW 11:28-30

8

Running a Check

Good chefs will tell you
that good meals are carefully orchestrated,
like good plays and good operas.
Food is meant to be enjoyed
not only by the mouth and the tastebuds
but also by the eyes, ears, nose, and fingers.

"Color combinations and shapes
are just as important
as correct temperature, textures, and aromas.
Even sounds are connected in our minds
with particular foods. Imagine how
the best chilled dill pickle would taste
if, when you bit into it, the crunchy sound
were missing."

LOUIS SZATHMARY

Praying—spiritual nourishment—
is similar to eating, physical nourishment.
It too involves the total person.
Our bodily posture, our breathing,
how we hold our hands, how we focus our eyes—
all of these things are important in prayer.
To ignore them
is to enter into prayer with a severe handicap.

This is why spiritual directors recommend
that occasionally we run a check
on the comportment of our body during prayer.

Here are some key areas to check on.

Is my back straight?

Believe it or not, an erect back is a good
way to cut down on or eliminate distractions.
There is no scientific data to explain this,
but it is a common experience of meditators.

Are my eyes at rest?

There are several ways to handle the eyes:
close them, allow them to remain open
and point straight ahead of you, unfocused,
or focus them on a cross
or a restful photograph.

Are my hands at rest?

Sometimes it helps to keep the hands apart,
resting them on the knees.
Sometimes it helps to cup or intertwine them,
resting them in your lap.
The important thing is to still them.

Is my breathing smooth and relaxed?

Don't strain it, but try to set up a rhythmic
pattern of inhalation and exhalation.

Finally, is my body at rest?

The less a body moves in prayer, usually,
the better.
At first it may be difficult to keep still,
but with time this will come about naturally.

*Our human efforts in prayer
may be likened to the efforts of a fisherman
casting a net into the sea.
Unless the net has been cast carefully,
the hope of success is small.*

Reflection

The soccer star Pele
used to prepare for games by stretching out
full-length on the floor.
Propping his feet up on a bench,
he would fold one towel under his head
and place a second towel over his eyes.

Then he would replay a happy memory.
The memory might be from his childhood,
when he played barefoot on Brazilian beaches.
Or he might recall a more recent event,
perhaps a winning goal he scored in a big game.
The exercise relaxed him not only physically
but also mentally.

The more important the game to be played,
the longer Pele drew out his replay.
When the New York Cosmos played Tampa Bay,
Pele ran his replay to nearly half an hour.
He then went out and mesmerized a crowd
of 60,000 fans by scoring three goals.

Now recall some happy memory from *your* past.
When and where did it take place?
What was it? How old were you?

"Lord . . .
I remember the days gone by;
I think about all that you have done,
I bring to mind all your deeds,
I lift up my hands to you in prayer. . . .
Remind me . . . of your constant love."
PSALM 143:5-8

9

Starting a Journal

Joan never knew her father.
He died when she was still quite young.
Her only concrete link with him
was a box of his belongings in the attic.
For years, they lay there untouched.
One day Joan decided to clean the attic.
She wrote later:

"I rediscovered the crate. . . .
I laid out the folders. . . .
Then I began to read. . . .

"I read a journal my father started at 17 . . .
he had left home . . .
and enrolled at Boston University.
By midwinter, he has worn out
his one pair of shoes and bought books
instead of a blanket. He drinks mugs of water
to still his hunger. A four-page entry
celebrating his discovery of great poets ends,
'I have not eaten today.'"
JOAN MILLS

People frequently start journals
when they begin some new experience.
Fifteen-year-old Scott started his journal
when he became terminally ill with leukemia.
Scott's journal entries range from happy ones
to depressing ones to thoughtful reflections.

When it seemed he might recover, he wrote:

"I remember the ride home. . . .
The trees, grass, birds, even the sun
seemed to greet me. . . .
For the first time in way over a month,
I was really, truly happy."

Commenting on love, Scott wrote:

"When you are very sick,
it helps to have someone hold your hand,
letting the glowing warmth of their love
for you trickle into you."
ELAINE IPSWITCH

Simply defined, a journal is a notebook
in which we write the thoughts and feelings
that all of us need to express
either in speech or in writing.
It isn't necessary to write every day,
or more than a few lines at a time.
What you write may not seem important
at the time, but it will later. For example:

A young man had given up meditation
after months of effort and mediocre success.
One night he stumbled upon his journal.
"Reading my journal," he said later,
"inspired me to start meditating again."

Over and above its many other values,
a prayer journal is a concrete manifestation
of a person's all-out, genuine commitment
to a program of daily meditation and prayer.

The most powerful journals
are usually those whose entries were made
while the emotions and ideas were white-hot.
"One note set down on the spot,"
wrote the English poet Thomas Gray,
"is worth a whole carload of later
reminiscences."

Reflection

In his book *Sadhana: A Way to God,*
Anthony de Mello has a fantasy contemplation.
I present it in a slightly adapted form.

Imagine you are sitting on a high mountain.
At the base of the mountain is a great city.
The sun is setting; the sight is spectacular.
Soon darkness comes;
the city is transformed into a sea of lights.
As you sit there, what are your feelings?
Soon you hear footsteps behind you,
the steps of a monk who lives on the mountain.
He pauses at your side and says: "If you go
down into the city tonight, you will find God."
Then, without explanation, he disappears.
Something tells you the monk is right.
You decide to go down into the city
to search for God.

Where will you look for him first? Why here?
How will you know it is God?

Jesus said:
*"I was hungry and you fed me,
thirsty and you gave me a drink;
I was a stranger and you received me . . .
naked and you clothed me;
I was sick and you took care of me,
in prison and you visited me. . . .
Whenever you did this for one of the least
important of these brothers of mine,
you did it for me!"*
MATTHEW 25:35-40

37

10

Using a Journal

Young Anne Frank began her journal
when her family went into hiding from the Nazis
in Amsterdam, Holland during World War II.

For two years they evaded the Nazis;
but then police found the hideout.
They confiscated everything of apparent value,
but they missed Anne's journal.

Anne explained a value of her journal:
"I can shake off everything if I write;
my sorrows disappear, my courage is reborn."

Eight months after her capture,
Anne died in Bergen-Belsen concentration camp.
Her journal has since been translated
into dozens of languages and made into a film.
A beautiful entry from the journal reads:

"It's really a wonder that I haven't dropped
all my ideals, because they seem so absurd
and impossible to carry out. Yet I keep them,
because in spite of everything
I still believe that people are really good
at heart. . . . If I look up into the heavens,
I think that it will all come right . . .
and that peace and tranquility will return."

A journal's main value
often lies not in the entries we make in it,

but in what takes place within us as we write.
Writing is a proven way of finding out
what is going on deep within us.
It helps us get in touch with our deeper,
unknown selves.
It tunes us in to the wordless conversation
going on in the sanctuary of our being
between God and ourselves.

A journal is valuable also
because it invites us to discipline ourselves.
It invites us to confront the same questions
Jesus put to his followers:

"Who do you say that I am?" Luke 9:20

*"Do you not believe . . . that I am in the Father
and the Father is in me?"* John 14:10

*"Will a person gain anything if he gains the
whole world but is himself lost . . . ?"* Luke 9:25

These are questions every Christian must face.
One way to face them is to pray over them
and write out our responses to Jesus.
It helps even more to share our responses
with a director or a small group of friends.

This kind of faith confrontation
is important, especially in our confused age.
It is even more important for people
trying to discover Jesus for the first time.

We must break away from the crowd,
go off alone with Jesus,
and listen as he asks us the same questions
that he asked his disciples:
"Simon, son of John, do you love me?" John 21:16

Reflection

"One night, about nine o'clock,
I was alone in my backyard shoveling snow.
We were going to flood it for ice skating.
After a while I began to feel really lonely,
sandwiched in between the garage on one side
and the house jutting out of the darkness
on the other side.
I decided to pause and take a break.

"I let myself fall back into the heavy snow.
It cushioned my fall and packed in around me.
I stared out from my snowy nest into the sky.
Every inch of it was filled with stars.

"Then, something strange happened.
I was still alone, but I didn't feel lonely.
I felt at one with everything and everyone,
especially all people—on Earth and, perhaps,
even on one of those stars up there.
Maybe, I thought, someone up there
was looking down on earth from his backyard
feeling the same way."

HIGH SCHOOL STUDENT: ADAPTED

"Praise the Lord from heaven,
you that live in the heights above. . . .
Praise him, sun and moon;
praise him, shining stars. . . .
Praise him . . . snow and clouds. . . .
Praise him . . . all peoples. . . .
Praise the Lord!"

PSALM 148

APPROACHES

"Heavenly Father!
When the thought of you awakes in our hearts,
let it not awake like a frightened bird
that thrashes about in fear,
but like a peaceful child
waking from sleep with a trusting smile."
SOREN KIERKEGAARD

11

Starting Point

When Jimmy Carter became president,
he placed a plaque on his White House desk.
It contained an old "Fisherman's Prayer":

"O God, thy sea is so great
and my boat is so small."

Some people hesitate to call it a prayer.
Actually, it reveals the basic starting point
for all prayer: a person standing consciously
in God's presence.

Standing consciously in God's presence
means standing before God as we are:
happy, bored, angry.
We do not try to kid God or ourselves
about our situation or how we feel about it.

We stand before God as a young soldier did
in Newfoundland one day:

"How lost and alone I felt—a boy of 17,
thousands of miles from anyone who loved me,
separated from my family and friends
by a vast sea and an unhappy life.

"One day I walked down
to the end of Main Street in Stephenville.
There a cliff dropped off sharply to the beach
and the Atlantic Ocean.

"I stood there,
my eyes fixed in the direction of home.
It gradually dawned on me that,
though I was lonely,
I never felt *completely* alone. Somehow,
I had always known that God was with me.

"At that moment,
standing on a cliff overlooking a vast ocean,
I knew that God would always be with me
despite my alienating ways, my wanderings,
and my sins."
DWAYNE SUMMERS

Standing consciously in God's presence
is the starting point of all meditation.
Concretely, this means calling to mind
that God is present with us.

From time to time,
God makes his presence felt by us.
When God does this, we merely rest there.
We do no more than remain in his presence.
We forget about the material
we were going to use for meditation.
We simply remain in God's presence
as long as he grants us this priceless gift.

On our part, any effort
to make ourselves feel God's presence
is nearly always wrong.
It cannot be wished or willed into being.
It is a gift from God.

Reflection

Imagine you are waiting for an elevator
on the tenth floor.
It comes; you enter and prepare to descend,
not to the bottom of a building
but into your inner self,
the deepest part of your being.

Imagine these are the feelings inside you
as the elevator starts to descend, floor by floor:

10 you feel yourself relax;
 9 you feel yourself relax even more;
 8 you feel all tension leave your body;
 7 you feel all worries leave your mind;
 6 you feel good all over;

 5 a deep peace fills your mind;
 4 a deep love fills your heart;
 3 a deep joy fills your soul;
 2 you feel something wonderful happening;
 1 the door opens; you stand in awe.

INSPIRED BY GEORGE MALONEY

"I saw the Lord.
He was sitting on his throne. . . .
Around him flaming creatures were standing. . . .
They were calling out to each other:

"'Holy, holy, holy!
The Lord Almighty is holy!'"
ISAIAH 6:1-3

12

Crossing Over

Standing consciously in God's presence
invites a revolution in our sense of reality.
A book seems more real than thought.
A heart seems more real than love,
sense reality more real than spirit reality.

To stand consciously in God's presence
is to ask faith to take us by the hand
and lead us across the narrow, dark tunnel
that links the worlds of sense and spirit.
Thus, both worlds become equally real to us.

Some people facilitate this
by putting themselves in the shoes of
biblical people whose faith allowed them
to cross back and forth with relative ease
between the two worlds. For example:

*"Whenever the people of Israel set up camp,
Moses would take the sacred Tent
and put it up some distance outside the camp. . . .
People would stand at the door of their tents
and watch Moses until he entered it.*

*"After Moses had gone in, the pillar of cloud
would come down . . . and the Lord
would speak to Moses from the cloud.
As soon as people saw the pillar of cloud . . .
they would bow down."*
EXODUS 33:7-11

Karl Barth likened the Bible reader
to someone looking from a tall building
down to a crowd of people in the street.
The people are gazing into the sky
at something hidden from the viewer by the roof.
They are captivated by something he doesn't see.

To stand consciously in God's presence
is to invite faith to open our "spiritual eyes"
to whatever it is that captivates these people.
This does not mean that we "feel" anything.
Feeling and *faith* are two different things,
as Keith Miller notes in *The Taste of New Wine:*

"I had been a spiritual sensualist,
always wanting to feel God's presence . . .
and being depressed when I didn't. . . .
So I tried this praying
whether I felt spiritual or not;
and for the first time in my life
found that we *can* live on raw faith. . . .
Often the very act of praying this way
brings later a closer sense of God's presence.

"And I realized a strange thing:
that if a person in his praying has the *feeling*
he doesn't need the *faith.*

"I began to feel very tender toward God
on those mornings during which I would pray
without any conscious sense of His presence.
I felt this way because at last
I was giving back to him the gift of faith."

A great saint used to make
"standing in the Lord's presence"
the body and heart of her daily meditation.
Recommending it to others, she wrote:

"Imagine this Lord himself at your side . . .
Stay with this good friend as long as you can . . .
You need not be concerned about conversing."
TERESA OF AVILA

Reflection

Imagine
your body relaxing and becoming very light.
Feel it float up into the air like a balloon.
Feel yourself soar through the air like a bird.
For about 20 minutes you soar along.

Finally, you slow down and return to earth.
You come to rest beside a beautiful lake
of fresh, clear, quiet water.
You plunge in for a delightful swim.

You emerge from the water
and lie down on the soft, green grass.
The sun dries your wet body.

You feel God's presence in the sun.
You feel his love in its warmth.
You wish you could lie here forever and ever,
bathed in God's presence and love.

"The Lord is my shepherd. . . .
He lets me rest in fields of green grass
and leads me to quiet pools of fresh water.
He gives me new strength. He guides me
in the right paths, as he has promised.
Even if I go through the deepest darkness,
I will not be afraid, Lord. . . .

"I know that your goodness and love
will be with me all my life;
and your house will be my home
as long as I live."
PSALM 23

13

Meditating

Baseball stars and race car champions
have given meditation an attractive new image.
Often, the question among star athletes is not
"Do you meditate?" but *"How* do you meditate?"

This leads to an important distinction.
In talking about this spiritual exercise
we can have in mind meditation as *pre-prayer*
and meditation as *prayer*.

Meditation as pre-prayer is an exercise
for tapping the fullness of human power
available to us.
Meditation as prayer is an exercise
for tapping the fullness of divine power
available to us.
The first does not necessarily involve faith
in God; the second does.

We call the first meditation as pre-prayer
because it prepares the spiritual athlete
mentally and physically for praying,
just as it prepares the physical athlete
mentally and physically for playing.

Meditation as pre-prayer
allows the body and the mind to slow down
and to relax sufficiently so that we can
enter God's presence consciously.
At this point, prayer becomes possible.

Normally, prayer takes three forms:
meditation—thinking about God;
contemplation—resting in God's presence;
conversation—talking with God.

Often, these three forms
occur intertwined in one and the same prayer,
like strands of wire in the same cable.
Consider this prayer experience:

"I was walking home one night quite late.
I happened to look up at the moon.
It was then that I started to think about God
and wonder what he was like.
Suddenly, the thought hit me that he made me.
The idea overwhelmed me—why, I'm not sure.
Anyway, I stopped dead in my tracks
and stood there, thinking and saying nothing.
After a few minutes—I'm not sure how long—
I thanked God for giving me life.
Then I continued on my way home."

Note all three prayer forms in the experience.

Meditation itself can assume many forms
(as we will see in the days ahead).
One popular form is to take an idea
and explore it in the presence of God.

For instance, take the idea of God himself.
A good God-meditation example is Psalm 139,
which explores God from three viewpoints:
his knowledge, his presence, his providence.

"Each time I visit my island
off the coast of Maine,
I fall in love with the sea again.
Now I don't know all of the sea—
wide areas of it will always be unknown to me–
but I know the sea.
It has a near range. It washes my island.
I can sit beside it . . . and sail over it,
and be sung to sleep by the music of it.
God is like that.
He is so great in His vastness
that we can think of Him only in symbolic terms,
but He has a near range."

HARRY EMERSON FOSDICK

Reflection

The sun was setting slowly over the Pacific.
I could hear the cry of sea gulls.
I could hear the pounding of the surf.
My thoughts leaped heavenward
to my Lord and creator:

"Lord . . .
you know me. You know everything I do;
from far away you understand all my thoughts.
You see me, whether I am working or resting;
you know all my actions.
Even before I speak,
you already know what I will say. . . .

"Where could I go to escape from you?
Where could I get away from your presence?
If I went up to heaven, you would be there;
if I lay down in the world of the dead,
you would be there. . . .
I could ask the darkness to hide me . . .
but even darkness is not dark for you,
and the night is as bright as day. . . .

"You created every part of me. . . .
When my bones were being formed,
carefully put together in my mother's womb,
when I was growing there in secret,
you knew that I was there—
you saw me before I was born.
The days allotted to me had all been recorded
in your book, before any of them ever began."
PSALM 139:1-16

14

Contemplating

Your head is a good place to launch prayer.
But that is all it is—a launching pad.

"If your prayer stays [in your head] too long
and doesn't move into the heart
it will gradually dry up
and prove tiresome and frustrating.
You must learn
to move out of the area of thinking and talking
and move into the area of . . . loving . . .
This is the area
where contemplation is born. . . ."
ANTHONY DE MELLO

Describing meditation, Thomas Keating says:

"One reflects on what one is reading
and hearing while turning it over in one's mind
in God's presence.
It gives rise to reactions in the will:
feelings of gratitude, petition, sorrow for sin.
Contemplation prayer is a more advanced stage
in which devotional thoughts are secondary.
Thoughts are laid to rest.
One sort of awaits and relishes God
in interior silence."

On this point, an old Sufi manuscript says:
"The moment the heart begins to recite,
the tongue should be silent."

How often have we heard an older person say:
"I find it impossible to pray as I used to."
The reason for this may be quite simple:
their prayer is in the contemplative stage.
They no longer need words to act as a key
to open the heart. The heart is already open.

Here, it is important to realize
that our prayer style tends to evolve with age.
Michael Lapierre traces the evolution:

"During childhood
recited prayer predominates . . .
words learned . . . from a book. . . .

"From adolescence to manhood
meditative prayer develops. . . .
We also find spoken prayer during this period. . . .
It may be the outburst of an emotion
of joy, praise, gratefulness, sorrow. . . .

"Finally, silent prayer
is the prayer of the mature man, whose soul
remains speechless in the presence of God,
aware of the inadequacy of whatever it may say."

To control distractions in this latter stage,
Thomas Keating gives simple but sound advice:

"Repeat a single word
which expresses your faith
or your surrendering to God, like 'Jesus,'
'love,' or whatever word is meaningful to you."

"We wonder
at towering mountains, crashing seas,
and orbiting stars—
but forget to wonder at ourselves."
ST. AUGUSTINE

Reflection

I dreamed
I was walking along the beach with the Lord,
and across the sky
flashed scenes from my life. For each scene
I noticed two sets of footprints in the sand;
one belonged to me, the other to the Lord.

When the last scene flashed before us
I looked back at the footprints in the sand.
I saw that many times along the path of life,
there was only one set of footprints.
I also noticed that it happened
at the lowest and saddest times in my life.
I questioned the Lord about it.

"Lord, you said that once I followed you,
you would walk with me all the way,
but I have noticed that during
the most troublesome times in my life,
there is only one set of footprints.
I don't understand why, in times
when I need you most, you would leave."

The Lord replied, "My precious child,
I would never leave you
during your times of trial and suffering.
When you see only one set of footprints,
it was then that I carried you."

AUTHOR UNKNOWN

*"The Lord, your God, carried you, as a man
carries his child, all along your journey."*
DEUTERONOMY 1:31 NAB

15

Conversing

Piri Thomas, an ex-pusher and attempted killer, describes the night his life changed:

"I went back to my cell . . .
I decided to make a prayer.
It had to be on my knees . . .
I couldn't play it cheap. . . .

"I knelt at the foot of the bed
and told God what was in my heart.
I made like he was there in the flesh . . .
I felt like I was someone
that belonged to someone who cared.
I felt like I could even cry if I wanted to,
something I hadn't been able to do for years."

As this episode shows, one way
to converse with God is to talk to him
as we would talk to our best friend.
We tell him about our doubts and dreams,
our difficulties and disappointments.

A "conversation guide" for talking to God
that many people find helpful
is to sit down with God, so to speak,
and do a "mental replay" of our day.

First, we identify and share with God
those events about which we feel most happy:

when we helped someone or were helped;
acted from principle, not from expediency,
enjoyed a special time with good friends.
We conclude by thanking God
for these high points in our day.

Next, we identify and share with God
those events about which we feel least happy:
when we turned aside from someone in need;
spoke harshly to another,
gave in to pettiness and jealousy.
We conclude by asking God
to forgive us these low points in our day.

Finally, we speak to God about tomorrow.
We preview any scheduled activities
that may need God's special help and guidance.
We conclude by asking God to help us
in these crucial points that lie ahead.

This way of talking to God provides
not only a framework for our prayer
but also a flexibility, lest it become routine.

Conversing with God involves dialogue.
It involves not only talking to God
but listening as God talks to us.

God does not talk to us in a vocal way.
He communicates to us in a spiritual way,
and at a level so deep within ourselves
that we would never know it existed
had he not declared himself to us there.

You are alone with your best friend.
Now tell this best friend about your life.
Tell him how much time you devote to yourself—
your work and your leisure;
how much time you give to helping others;
how much time you devote to him.
After this ask him:
"Lord, what do you think of my life?"
Then, just listen.

Reflection

Relax completely.
Set up a pattern of slow, rhythmic breathing.

As you inhale, imagine God's powerful love
flowing into your body
through the pores of your skin.

As this love flows into your body,
imagine that it remains trapped inside you,
building up the store of love within you.

Imagine your body becoming a great lamp,
radiating love to the world about you.

Now just rest there,
allowing God's love to build up inside you
and radiate from you to all the world.

Jesus said:
"I love you just as the Father loves me. . . .
Love one another, just as I love you!"
JOHN 15:9, 15:12

Let this teaching of Jesus' penetrate you.
Then, when you are ready
mentally, visit any person you know
who seems to have special need of God's love.
Place both your hands on that person's head.
As you exhale,
imagine God's love flowing out from your body,
through your hands, into the other person.
Stay with the person as long as you feel
you are needed.

16

Praying from Print

A young man writes of his mother's death:

"I was bewildered and lost.
I missed my mother immensely.
Everything she ever touched became precious.
Then, one day, my eyes fell upon a card
under the glass top on my dresser.
I recalled seeing it there
for the first time a few weeks earlier.
But I had not bothered to read it.
Now, I pulled it out and read:

Romans 8:28

'For ev'ry pain we must bear,
For ev'ry burden, ev'ry care,

there's a reason.

'For ev'ry grief that bows the head,
For ev'ry teardrop that is shed,

there's a reason.

'For ev'ry hurt, for ev'ry plight,
For ev'ry lonely, pain-racked night,

there's a reason.

'But if we trust God, as we should,
It will work out for our good.

He knows the reason.'

"As I sat there, I could picture my mother
coming into my room and slipping the card

beneath the glass, as if to say:
'It's all right; he knows the reason.'"

HIGH SCHOOL STUDENT: ADAPTED

Sometimes we find printed prayers
that speak to us in a special way—
almost as though they were written for us.
These are prayers
that we should save or copy in a journal.
This makes them "our" prayers.
Such prayers act not only as *model prayers*
but also as *prayer models.*

A model prayer is simply a prayer
that we like as it is. We enjoy praying it
just as we enjoy listening to certain songs.
A prayer model, on the other hand,
is a prayer that we follow,
much as a backpacker follows a trail
in the wilderness.
Like the backpacker, we don't hug the trail,
but move off it occasionally
to enjoy an exciting view
or something beautiful along the way.

Printed prayers, like wilderness trails,
act as guides to keep us from getting lost
or traveling in circles.

Like good friends, printed prayers
are always there when we need them,
in every situation, every hour of the day.

*"We know that in all things
God works for good with those who love him."*
ROMANS 8:28

Reflection

"We had been canoeing
in the Canadian wilderness for over a week
and were tired and in need of rest.
Then, as though the Lord himself
were taking special care of us,
we spotted a small trapper's cabin
sitting back in a wooded thicket
about twenty yards from the bank of the river.
We beached our canoe
and headed up the bank toward the cabin.
The door was open; the cabin was empty,
except for an open Bible on a bunk bed.
Laid across the pages was this note:
Your cabin saved my life.
I had taken seriously ill and needed shelter.
Your cabin provided it.
I cannot repay you with money,
only with God's blessing.
Read the passage below this card.
I lifted the card and read.

"Then the King will say . . .
Come and possess the kingdom . . .
I was hungry and you fed me,
thirsty and you gave me a drink;
I was a stranger and you received me . . .
I was sick and you took care of me . . .
Whenever you did this for one of these . . .
you did it for me." Matthew 25:34-40
JOHN PIANO

17

Praying from Memory

Dr. Sheila Cassidy
was arrested and tortured in Chile
for treating a political enemy of the state.
Describing the ordeal, she wrote:

"After four days of physical pain, . . .
I was left completely alone in a small room. . . .
I was filled with an enormous amount of fear. . . .
And I remembered
the prayer Dietrich Bonhoeffer wrote
while he was awaiting execution . . .

"'In me there is darkness.
But with Thee there is light. . . .
Lord, whatsoever this day may bring,
Thy name be praised.'"

Dr. Cassidy's recourse to memorized prayer
fits a pattern experienced by others.
In *When Iron Gates Yield,*
Geoffrey Bull credits his survival in prison
to the strength he found in repeating,
over and over,
Scripture he had memorized in his youth.

Seventeen-year-old Joni Eareckson
had similar recourse to memorized prayer
after a diving accident in the Chesapeake Bay.
Fully conscious but totally paralyzed
(as she remains today),
she was rushed to a hospital. She says:

"I could not collect my thoughts
enough to pray.
I clung to memorized promises from the Bible."

People sometimes refer to "memorized praying"
as "praying by heart."
This is an excellent description
of what memorized praying is all about.
It is letting the words of a remembered prayer
descend from the head into the heart,
where they acquire a deeper meaning
and speak to us—or let us speak to God—
in a deeper or more profound way.

People sometimes complain
that memorized prayer is impersonal prayer,
because the words are predetermined for us.

This is a misunderstanding of the situation.
It is like saying that food is impersonal
because it is predetermined in taste.

The personal dimension of memorized prayer
comes not from the words
prayed by the person,
but from the person praying the words.

No two people
pray the same words in the same way.
The words, then,
return to God restyled and restamped
with the unique personality of the person
who prayed them.

*Jesus taught the use of memorized prayers
by personal example. On the cross
he prayed Psalm 22: "My God, my God,
why did you abandon me?" Mark 15:33
As death came, he prayed Psalm 31: "Father!
In your hands I place my spirit!" Luke 23:46*

Reflection

Teaching his students how to recite a prayer
"printed" in the memory
or printed on the page of a prayerbook,
a rabbi said:
"Teach the heart to hear and to repeat
the words the mouth says."

This means reciting the prayer
while attending thoughtfully to its meaning.

If we become distracted while praying,
we return to the place of the distraction
and resume again.
When we have completed the prayer,
we pause in silence
and invite God to respond
in whatever way he might choose.

Now pray the following prayer in this way:

"Lord,
teach me to be generous.

"Teach me
to serve you as you deserve;
to give and not to count the cost;
to fight and not to heed the wounds;
to toil and not to seek for rest;
to labor and not to ask for reward;

except to know
that I am doing your will."

IGNATIUS OF LOYOLA

18

Praying Out Loud

"Once I read passages
from Will Shakespeare's *Twelfth Night*
to a group of college English teachers.
Afterward a young instructor confronted me.
'That wasn't quite fair,' he said. 'You edited
those passages to make them livelier.'

"'But I didn't skip a word,' I protested.
'Whatever made you think that I did?'

"'Well,' he replied simply,
'this is the first time
I ever completely understood the play.'
I feel certain
that this new appreciation of the drama was
inspired by the enjoyment of hearing it read."
CHARLES LAUGHTON

Other people report
a similar new appreciation of the gospel
when they read aloud sentences from it
to meditate on during prayer.

Still others report
that speaking out loud to God in prayer
results in a new understanding of prayer.

Recently, I was walking down Halsted Street
past the University of Illinois Circle Campus.
A shabbily-dressed young man
was walking slowly a few yards ahead of me.

As I approached, I could hear him talking.
I became somewhat embarrassed
as I heard what he was saying:

"What do you think
Jesus, your Lord and Savior, would say?
You know what he would say!
And what are you going to do about it?
Well, you'd better do something,
and you'd better do it soon!"

What impressed me
was that he was perfectly sober and sincere.
And he didn't care who heard him.
He was lost in serious reflection.
I envied him as I turned toward home.

A few days later, another young man
came to my office to talk about his prayer life.
He was all excited:

"I've just had a great breakthrough," he said.
"I was all alone at home last night,
so I decided to pray to God out loud.
The experience was overpowering.
After a while I stopped talking
and conversed silently with God in a way
that I have never been able to do before."

Reading out loud or praying out loud
heightens our sense of involvement and reality.
We begin to experience the gospel and prayer
in a whole new way.

"Reading aloud
suggests that what is being read is precious.
Perhaps that is a quality we need to recapture
in a deliberate and childlike way. "
EVA LEWIS PERERA

Reflection

Pray aloud the following prayer.
Pause between sentences
to let the ideas sink in and touch your heart.
Do not be in a hurry to move on.
Stay with a thought
as long as it continues to touch and move you.

"Jesus, Lord of the sea and winds,
calm the storm when we are frightened.
"Jesus, Lord of the loaves and fishes,
be our food when we are hungry.
"Jesus, Lord of the lambs and flocks,
seek us out when we are lost.

"Jesus, Lord of signs and wonders,
show yourself when we have doubts.
"Jesus, Lord of the blind and lame,
take our hand when we grow weak.
"Jesus, Lord of fields and flowers,
care for us when others can't.

"Jesus, Lord of all that lives,
be our God; we are your people."

"Jesus said . . . ,
'So I tell you
not to worry. . . .
Your Father
is pleased
to give you the Kingdom. . . .
Your heart
will always be
where your riches are.'"
LUKE 12:22, 32-34

19

Praying for Others

"Prayer is the highest energy of which the
mind is capable," wrote Samuel Taylor Coleridge.

Alexis Carrel, Nobel Prize-winning surgeon,
testified similarly:

"Prayer is the most
powerful form of energy one can generate.
The influence of prayer
on the human mind and body
is as demonstrable as that of secreting glands.
Prayer is a force as real as terrestrial gravity.
It supplies us with a flow of sustaining power."

Elsewhere Carrel said:

"When we pray we link ourselves
with the inexhaustible motive power
which spins the universe. . . .
We ask that a part of this power
be apportioned to our needs."

But the "prayer of petition,"
which Jesus taught and practiced so naturally,
is a problem for many modern Christians.
"What does it mean?" they ask. "Does God
modify his acts because we ask him to?"

The answer seems obvious.
God doesn't need human wisdom to guide him.
Nor does he need human persuasion

to lead him to what is good and right.
Why, then, did Jesus teach us to pray?

Blaise Pascal,
the 17th-century French mathematician,
answered the question this way:
"Prayer is one of the ways that God
chose to share his infinite power with us."
Just as his gift of intelligence gives us power,
so his gift of prayer gives us power.

In other words,
God set up the universe in such a way
that we can influence it
not only by the exercise of human intelligence
but also by the exercise of human prayer.

God has made us more than spectators
to his creative power; we also share in it.
This is part of what it means
to be made in the "image and likeness of God."

Alexis Carrel summed up the role of prayer
this way:

"Prayer is a mature activity
indispensable
to the fullest development of personality.
Only in prayer do we achieve
that complete and harmonious assembly
of body, mind, and spirit
which gives the frail human reed
its unshakeable strength."

*When all life's mysteries are unveiled
and everything made known, we will probably see
that those who advanced our world most
were not those who excited it with dazzling feats,
but those who energized it with their prayers.*

Reflection

Imagine you are seated
on a Galilean hillside in the time of Jesus.
It is a lovely spring day.
Everywhere you look, you see people.
Suddenly, a hush falls upon the crowd.
A man with a striking appearance stands up.
In a strong, captivating voice, he says,

"When you pray,
do not use a lot of meaningless words,
as the pagans do,
who think that God will hear them
because their prayers are long. . . .
Your Father already knows what you need
before you ask him.
This, then, is how you should pray:

"'Our Father in Heaven:
May your holy name be honored;
may your Kingdom come;
may your will be done
on earth as it is in heaven.
Give us today the food we need.
Forgive us the wrongs we have done,
as we forgive the wrongs
that others have done to us.
Do not bring us to hard testing,
but keep us safe from the Evil One'. . . .

"Ask, and you will receive;
seek, and you will find;
knock, and the door will be opened to you."

MATTHEW 6:7-13, 7:7

79

SUPPORTS

*Corrie ten Boom and another prisoner
during World War II used to risk punishment
by walking about camp at night, praying:*

*"In that cold darkness,
Betsie and I walked with the Lord
and talked with the Lord.
Betsie said something, I said something,
then the Lord said something.
How? I don't know,
but we both understood what he said."*

20

Praying with Others

Monks in some eastern and western traditions
pray together in a common meditation hall.
Praying together like this gives them support
in their meditation commitment.

Small "prayer groups"
perform a similar function for many Christians
who have begun daily meditation programs.

Meeting together on a weekly basis
gives them an excellent opportunity, also,
to share and discuss common problems.
To find or form such a group is a treasure.

George Anderson
describes such a "prayer-discussion group"
that formed in the maximum security prison
at Riker's Island, New York:

"We would start
by reading parables like the good Samaritan
or Christ's washing the disciples' feet.
Then the inmates would reflect on the message.

"One evening we had a moving illustration
of how deeply the theme was understood.
Richard, an imate
from a section for mentally disturbed,
was with us for the first time. . . .

"It was a windy evening in March.
There was little heat in the room.
An inmate sitting opposite Richard
having come only in a T-shirt and trousers,
was shivering.
Richard had come with his shoulders wrapped
in two blankets.
Then while we were discussing the idea of
helping each other, Richard suddenly got up,
walked to the other inmate,
and put one of his blankets around him."

Sometimes the prayer level
reached in these small groups is profound.
One writer attempts to explain why:

"Most people
who have taken part in group prayer
will have sensed the deep interior silence
that sometimes enshrouds the whole gathering
as though the Spirit were palpably present.
This, I believe,
is a type of communal contemplation,
a form of meditation that is
particularly marked in a community of love.
Here it is not only the individual
but also the group that relishes an obscure
sense of enveloping presence."
WILLIAM JOHNSTON

Each group develops its own prayer style.
Groups, like individuals, must experiment
with time, place, and method.

Reflection

Imagine you and some close friends
decide to camp out at night on a beach.
You arrive before dark, build a beautiful fire,
and watch the sun sink below the horizon.

Soon the moon comes up,
throwing a shimmering silver carpet
across the quiet surface of the lake.
Overhead, millions of stars look down on you.

It is a magnificent night
and you lie around the fire doing nothing.
You are just happy to be together
enjoying each other's presence under the stars.

Your conversation, if you can call it that,
goes deeper than spoken words.
There is a special feeling present
that allows you to understand one another
without speaking.

"How wonderful it is, how pleasant,
for God's people
to live together in harmony!"
PSALM 133:1

"The Lord takes pleasure in his people. . . .
Let God's people rejoice in their triumph
and sing joyfully all night long. . . ."
"Praise the Lord!"

PSALM 149:4-5, 149:9

21

Praying with Wholeness

Thoreau said of his wilderness cabin:

"I had three chairs in my house,
one for solitude, two for friendship,
three for society."

Thoreau's terse comment spotlights
the three levels of our human personality:
personal, interpersonal, and communal.

Our psychological wholeness as persons
depends on how well we attend to each level.
If we respect the needs of each level,
we will grow in psychological wholeness.
If we don't, we will be stunted accordingly.

What is true of our psychological lives
is true, also, of our spiritual lives.

Concretely and ideally,
this means that our prayer lives should include:
times when we pray alone,
times when we pray with friends (or family),
and times when we pray with the community,
as at weekly worship services.

No one level can make up adequately
for the needs of another level.
All three call for personalized attention.

Jesus showed concern
for all three levels of human personality.

Concerning the *personal* level,
Jesus himself prayed in solitude. Mark 1:35
He also taught his followers to pray this way:
*"Go to your room, close the door, and pray
to your Father, who is unseen."* Matthew 6:6

Concerning the *interpersonal* level,
Jesus himself prayed with close friends:
*"Jesus took Peter, John, and James with him
and went up a hill to pray."* Luke 9:28
He also taught his followers
to pray this way, assuring them:
*"Where two or three come together in my name,
I am there with them."* Matthew 18:20

Finally, concerning the *communal* level,
Luke writes of Jesus: *"On the Sabbath he
went as usual to the synagogue."* Luke 4:16
Jesus also taught his followers
to pray as a community:

*"He took a piece of bread, gave thanks to God,
broke it, and gave it to [his apostles], saying,
'This is my body, which is given for you.
Do this in memory of me.'
In the same way, he gave them the cup
after the supper."* Luke 22:19-20

Thus, Jesus provided for spiritual nourishment
of each level of our human personality.

*Seeing the three tribes praying together
made the old chief recall his boyhood,
when he had sat by the river watching one tribe
wash the blood of the other two tribes
from their bodies and spears.
Now the old chief understood, as never before,
the meaning of Christianty: God calling us,
through Jesus, to live as a family.*

Reflection

"I had just finished my paper route.
It was Easter morning and I was walking home.

"As I passed St. Gall's church,
the sun was coming up.
I had no intention of going in for mass,
because I was in the midst
of a teenage rejection of the church.

"Then it happened!
I turned around just as the sun
struck the silver cross in front of the church.
I couldn't take my eyes off
the fiery brightness. I was overcome
by a sense of what the apostles must have felt
2,000 years ago on this same morning.
This feeling moved me deeply.

"An unseen force seemed to take hold of me,
directing my feet up the steps.
I opened the door, went in, and knelt down.
For the first time in a long time, I prayed.
For the first time
I understood what Easter was all about."

HIGH SCHOOL STUDENT: ADAPTED

"O God . . .
you have rescued me . . .
and kept me from defeat. . . .
In the shadow of your wings I find protection. . . .
Your constant love reaches the heavens;
your faithfulness touches the skies."

PSALMS 56:13; 57:1, 10

22

Reading the Bible

After a brush with death, a young man
decided to live a more Christian life.
He had no idea, however, what this involved.
He tried several approaches
but something important seemed to be missing.
He writes:

"Finally one day I met a layman
whose life had a power and a concern in it
which I knew instinctively were the things
my Christian life desperately lacked. . . .

"I asked this man what he considered to be the
most important discipline of his Christian life.
He pointed out
that reading the Scriptures every day
and having a specific time of prayer
for the cultivation
of a real and dynamic relationship with Christ
were the two things which had become
most meaningful and real for him."

KEITH MILLER

I have always been struck
by the order of the man's instruction:
reading the Scriptures and *then* prayer.
After years of trying to help people pray,
I have come to the conclusion
that reading the Bible faithfully each day
is the best single aid to learning to pray.

The first thing to keep in mind
is that we don't read the Bible
in the same way we read other books.
The Bible isn't *another* book; it is God's book.

This does not mean we ignore the fact
that the words and expressions in the Bible
are those of human authors
and mirror the author's backgrounds.

It does mean that we must be on our guard
lest the human words and expressions
distract us from God's word.
An illustration might help.
Recall Barth's comparison
that reading the Bible is like
looking out the window of a tall building
down to a crowd of people in the street.
The crowd is staring up at something
hidden from our view by the roof.

Developing the image, Frederick Buechner
writes that interpreting the Bible
is like reading the faces of the crowd and,
through them, seeing what the people see.
To do this, we don't look *at* the window—
dirtied and cracked by time—but *through* it.

In other words, when we read the Bible,
we don't let ourselves get sidetracked
by human words and ways of saying things.
Rather, we look *beyond* them to God's word,
of which they are but vehicles.

One way to start reading the Bible
is to start with Mark's gospel, the action gospel,
called by some the "Gospel of Jesus-on-the-Go."
A trait of Mark's
is to pose questions, leaving them unanswered.
When Jesus expels a demon, onlookers ask,
"What can this mean?"
When Jesus calms the sea, followers ask:
"Who can this be?"

Reflection

A plane carrying 30,000 letters to soldiers
crashed in 40 feet of water off Newfoundland.
At considerable risk to their own lives,
divers recovered the canvas bags of mail.

Why this concern for the letters?
Experience shows that soldiers cope better
with food shortages than with mail shortages.

One way to read the Bible is to view it
as a love letter of a Father to his children.
This creates an ideal mood for reading it.
Mortimer Adler tells why:

"There is only one situation I can think of
in which people make an effort to read better
than they usually do.
When they are in love and reading a love
letter, they read for all they are worth. . . .
They may even take the punctuation
into account."

In this spirit, consider these words in Mark:

"A crowd . . . said to [Jesus],
'Look, your mother and your brothers. . . .'
Jesus answered,
'Who is my mother? Who are my brothers?'
He looked at the people sitting around him
and said,
'Look! Here are my mother and my brothers!
Whoever does what God wants him to do
is my brother, my sister, my mother.'"
MARK 3:32-35

23

Understanding the Bible

A patient saw a Bible on his doctor's desk.
"Do you, a psychiatrist, read that?"
"I not only read it,"
said the psychiatrist, "I study it!"
He cited Jesus' teaching:
"Love your neighbor as yourself."

"That teaching is remarkable," he said,
"in its recognition that self-love and other-love
are both necessary for emotional health."
He noted further that low self-love
is one of the commonest psychic ailments.
Often this lack of self-love arises from
a person's past mistakes in conduct.
He then made this application:

"Suppose a woman
comes to me weighted down with guilt.
I can't undo the things she has done.
But perhaps I can help her to understand
why she did them and how the mechanism
of her conscience . . . is paralyzing her.
And I can urge her to read and reread
the story of the Prodigal Son.
How can anyone feel permanantly condemned . . .
in a world where this magnificent promise
comes ringing down the centuries,
the promise that love
is stronger than any mistake or error?"
SMILEY BLANTON

But the Bible
is more than a guide to emotional health.
It is a guide to faith and life in Jesus.
"I write," says John, *"that you may believe
that Jesus is the Messiah, the Son of God,
and that through your faith in him
you may have life."* John 20:31

But faith and life in Jesus
are not just a matter of reading the Bible.
They are also a matter of God's initiative.
In other words, God speaks through the Bible
in his own time and in his own way.

An example will illustrate.

One day Madame Chiang Kai-shek,
wife of Taiwan's famous general and leader,
was reading the Bible passage
where the soldier pierces the side of Jesus.

Although she had read the passage often,
she had never been moved, especially, by it.
This time, however, she cried.
Her tears sprang from both grief and relief—
grief for her sins
and relief that Jesus had died for them.
She said later that her crying
was even more unusual, because as a child,
she had been trained not show emotion.

Like prayer, reading the Bible fruitfully
combines our effort and God's initiative.
We cast the net, but God gives the catch.

*The way to read the Bible
is not to stand outside it as a spectator
but to enter into it as a participant.*

Reflection

Imagine
you are in Jerusalem on Good Friday.
You have just witnessed Jesus' trial.
Everything is over but the execution.
Now it begins.

The soldiers lead Jesus away.
A large crowd follows.

Some women are in the crowd.
They are weeping for Jesus.
Jesus says: *"Do not weep for me.*
Weep for yourselves and for your children."

Two criminals are with Jesus.
They too are to be crucified.

Soon, all arrive at Golgotha.
There they crucify Jesus.

They crucify the criminals also—
one at Jesus' right,
the other at Jesus' left.

Jesus prays: *"Father, forgive them; . . ."*

At noon, the sun grows dark.
Jesus cries out: *"Father,*
into your hands I commend my spirit."

A soldier cries out:
"Clearly this man was the Son of God!"

LUKE 23:26-36, and MARK 15:39, NAB

24

Praying the Bible

The Swedish film *Elvira Madigan*
begins with the statement that it is
the true love story of a young acrobat
and a soldier who were tragically killed.
Why did the director tell us this in advance?

He wanted us to view the film differently
from the way we normally view films.
He wanted us to focus on the couple's love
rather than on the film's plot.

Reading the Bible is something like this.
The biblical writers wanted us to read it
differently from the way we read other books.

In fact, there are many people who say:
"You can't really read the Bible;
you can only meditate or pray it."

There is much truth in this statement.
The Bible resists the casual reader
and yields only to the prayerful searcher.

Ignatius of Loyola suggested to his students
that they imagine themselves present
at the gospel events they read.
In other words,
they were to experience with their imaginations
the sights, sounds, and feelings
described or suggested in the events.

Take the crucifixion of Jesus.
Imagine you are one of the 20 or 30 soldiers
on duty at the execution site.

What do you see?

Three men hanging awkwardly on crosses.
The sky growing darker by the minute.
Flashes of lightning scattering onlookers.

What do you smell?

The scent of rain in the air.
Sweaty bodies and sweat-soaked clothes.
The smell of blowing dust.

What do you feel?

The air growing cooler.
Blowing sand, stinging your face.

What do you hear?

People shouting. Jesus crying out;
the crowd growing still.
The Roman soldier's awed voice:
"Clearly this man was the Son of God!"

Conclusion:

What thoughts go through your mind
as you stand there looking at Jesus?
Speak those thoughts to Jesus.

"To be ignorant of the Scriptures is to be ignorant of Christ."
ST. JEROME

Reflection

"There comes a time
when man must face life alone,
alone on a cross . . . alone on a city street
or alone in the hours of pain
which close out everyone else.
There comes a time
when a man knows his life can no longer
be repaired . . .

"There comes a time
when there is only God and only faith in him,
nothing else, no one else.
Jesus knew this on the cross."
ANTHONY PADOVANO

"Jesus cried in a loud voice,
'Eloi, Eloi, lama sabachthani?'
which means,
'My God, my God, why have you forsaken me?'
A few of the bystanders who heard it
remarked, 'Listen! He is calling on Elijah!'
Someone ran off,
and soaking a sponge in sour wine,
stuck it on a reed to try to make him drink.
The man said,
'Now let us see whether Elijah comes
to take him down.'

"Then Jesus,
uttering a loud cry, breathed his last."

MARK 15:34-37 NAB

CHALLENGES

"Happy is the person
who remains faithful under trials,
because when he succeeds in passing such a test,
he will receive as his reward
the life
which God has promised to those who love him."
JAMES 1:12

25

Feeling of Failure

Columbus wrote in his journal
that as his ship sailed past La Rabida
his crew could hear the monks on land
chanting their morning prayers.

Columbus's crew enjoyed the first weeks at sea.
But as the weeks passed, the picture changed.
Not one of Columbus's sailors had been more
than a few hundred miles from shore.
Now they were thousands of miles from home—
and still going. Fear gripped the crew.
We can picture Columbus alone in his cabin.
Staring down at the last entry in his journal,
he asks himself: "Have I failed?"

This picture also relates to the person
who has set out to voyage to God in prayer.
A day comes when he stares at the wall
and asks himself: "Have I failed?"

The feeling of having failed at prayer
shadowed the lives of the greatest saints.
After his conversion, Ignatius of Loyola
enjoyed praying in the caves of Montserrat.
Then, suddenly, his spiritual springtime
became a bitter winter.
All enjoyment of spiritual things fled him.
When he prayed in the caves of Montserrat,
he no longer felt God's presence.
His heart seemed to turn to ice.

To try to win the return of God's grace,
Ignatius decided to go on an eight-day fast.
But it didn't help. He prayed desperately:

"Hasten, Lord, to help me,
for I find no aid in people or in things.
If there were a dog I could pursue for help,
I would do it."

Then, just as suddenly as it had disappeared,
the spiritual springtime appeared again.

Voyaging to God in prayer,
as noted earlier, is not simply a matter
of effort and perseverance.
This is only half of the picture.
Prayer is also—above all—a gift from God.
And God gives according to his own wisdom.
He knows what is best for us,
and he will do what is best for us.

When we pray,
we are like the father of the runaway son
in Jesus' parable of the prodigal son.
The father could not force his son's return.
He could only wait for him and trust.

Voyaging to God in prayer is like that.
All we can do is wait for God, trust in God,
and persevere in our prayer discipline.
If we do this, God will certainly come.

Reflection

When I was a little boy
my mother used to read to me.
One of my favorite selections was a poem
entitled "The Acorn and the Pumpkin."

It concerned a young man
who walked outside one day to meditate.
He came to a field of ripe pumpkins.
In the field was a huge acorn tree.

The young man meditated on the tiny acorns
hanging down from the huge tree limbs.
Then he meditated on the huge pumpkins
fastened to the tiny vines.
"God blundered," the young man reflected.
"He should have put the tiny acorns
on the tiny vines
and the huge pumpkins on the huge limbs."

Then the young man lay down under the tree
and fell fast asleep.
A few minutes later, he was awakened
by a tiny acorn bouncing off his nose.
The young man rubbed his bruised nose
and thought: "Maybe God was right after all."

*"What seems to be God's foolishness
is wiser than human wisdom."*
I CORINTHIANS 1:25

26

Waiting and Watching

Waiting at a traffic light irritates us
because we can't make it change.
Waiting for an appointment annoys us
because we can't speed up the clock.
Waiting for a bus bothers us
because we cannot control its movement.
Prayer is something like this.

"I am no longer in control when I pray.
God is control. He will come
when he thinks it is time to come.

"Prayer is the courage to listen,
to give up self-determination. . . .
It implies waiting—as before any birth—
in darkness and expectancy."
PETER VAN BREEMAN

The posture we must assume in prayer
is best described by the Hebrew psalmist:

"I trust in the Lord;
my soul trusts his word.
My soul waits for the Lord
more than sentinels wait for the dawn."
PSALM 130:5-6 NAB

Waiting is just one side of the prayer coin.
The other side is watching and listening.
The watching and listening, however,
is done not with the eyes and ears of the body,

but with the eyes and ears of the heart.
And sometimes they grow weary and wander.
What should we do when this happens?
St. Francis de Sales gives this reply:

"Bring your wayward heart back home quietly.
Return it tenderly to its Master's side,
If you did nothing else during prayer
but return your heart
continually and patiently to the Master's side
your time of prayer would be well spent."

This leads to an all-important point.
Some people catalog the "benefits" of prayer:
it gives strength in times of trouble;
it gives peace in times of turmoil;
it gives insight into life and into ourselves.
Last but not least, God answers our prayers.

These are all excellent reasons for praying,
but they are secondary to the main one.

Prayer is its own end: It is loving God.
Prayer is an expression of love—
pure and complete in itself.

"This does not say
that prayer has no fruitful effects,
but only that its 'fruitfulness'
cannot be the end of prayer.
A friendship can offer many 'useful' benefits
but if they are the sole purpose of the
friendship then there is no friendship at all."
PETER VAN BREEMAN

"Tears may flow at night,
But joy comes in the morning."
PSALM 30:5

Reflection

An early TV star framed this saying
and hung it up in his office:

"The fire, Lord,
not the scrap heap."

"I hung it there to remind me of a story.
There was once a blacksmith
who had great faith in God
in spite of a lot of sickness in his life.
An unbeliever asked him one day
how he could go on trusting in a God
who let him suffer.

"'When I make a tool,'
the blacksmith answered, 'I take
a piece of iron and put it into the fire.
Then I strike it on the anvil
to see if it will take temper. If it does,
I can make a useful article out of it.
If not, I toss it on the scrap heap.'"
ARTHUR GODFREY

"Be glad . . .
of the many kinds of trials you suffer.
Their purpose is to prove
that your faith is genuine.
Even gold, which can be destroyed,
is tested by fire;
and so your faith,
which is much more precious than gold,
must also be tested, so that it may endure."
I PETER 1:6-7

27

Praying and Living

In *How to Meditate,* Lawrence Le Shan
recalls an ancient story about a monk
who prayed many years for a vision from God.
After he had almost given up, it came.
The monk's soul soared with joy and peace.

Suddenly, the monastery bell rang,
indicating that it was time
to feed the poor at the gate of the monastery.
It was the old monk's turn to share with them
whatever food was on hand that day.
The monk was torn between his vision
and his earthy occupation.
Before the echo of the bell had faded,
the bearded monk made the difficult choice.
He left the vision to feed the beggars.

Nearly an hour later, he returned to his room.
As he opened the door, he fell to his knees.
For there in his room was the same vision.
As he bowed his head, the vision said to him:
"Had you not gone, I would not have stayed."

We can't compartmentalize life and prayer.
In the words of earthy Josh Billings,
we can't "pray cream and live skim milk."
Prayer does not take place in a vacuum.
It is not an escape from life,
but a preparation for it.

It is not an isolated island in the sea of life,
but a celebration of life.

"People who only know how to think about God
during certain fixed periods of the day
will never get very far in the spiritual life.
In fact they will not even think of Him
in the moments they have religiously marked off
for 'mental prayer.'"

THOMAS MERTON

The reason is clear.
Our habitual lifestyle sets up a momentum
that permeates and influences our prayer life.
If our life attitudes are negative and askew,
we will find it next to impossible to pray
on a daily basis.

For example, do we view God
as our judge or as our Father?
Do we view ourselves as people
worthy of being loved
or as people unworthy of it?
Do we view others as competitors
or as brothers and sisters?
Do we view the gospel as narratives
about someone past
or as insights into someone with us now?
Do we view life as a home or as a road?

Our attitudes toward life are inseparably
interlaced with our attempts to pray daily.

Learn from the rock climber
who moves gracefully, almost mysteriously:

"Never glancing down,
he sometimes stops to shake out his hand,
then climbs on. Higher and higher. . . .

"One must be near the mountains to understand it,
one must be thrilled by them. . . .

"Climbing is more than a sport.
it is an entry into myth.
For those irresistibly drawn to it, it becomes a life."
JAMES SALTER

Reflection

"One day I found myself depressed and lonely
in a little cabin in northern California.
I turned my questioning to God. . . .
This time I really wanted to know the truth.
I was willing to do anything God said . . .
Then he spoke to me . . . He simply told me,
'Practice my word. Act on my word, even if
you don't understand exactly what it means.
When you act on my word
you'll come to understand its meaning.' . . .

"That one simple statement God made to me
began to dominate my thinking.
Though I stumbled around at first . . .
my life with God was moving forward
in a significant direction.
God brought my family back together
and healed my wife and children
of the damage I had inflicted on them. . . .
"God's intervention
and my own painful experience
had taught me a lesson I would never forget:
I learned to hear the word and to act on it."
JIM DURKIN

Jesus said:
*"So if you are about to offer your gift to God
at the altar and there you remember
that your brother has something against you,
leave . . . and make peace with your brother,
and then come back and offer your gift to God."*
MATTHEW 5:23-24

28

Keeping It Simple

"The Three Hermits" is a Russian folk tale
about three monks living on an island.
According to Leo Tolstoy, who tells the story,
they were so simple, their only prayer was:

"We are three;
you are three;
have mercy on us."

Miracles sometimes occurred during the prayer.

When the bishop heard about the monks,
he went to visit them.
He hoped to teach them to pray
in a more appropriate way.

After he had finished instructing the monks,
the bishop set sail again for the mainland.
Suddenly,
he saw a ball of light chasing his boat.
It was the three monks
running across the water.

When they reached the boat, they said:
"We have forgotten a part of your instruction
and want to check it with you."

The bishop shook his head humbly and said:
"Forget what I taught you
and continue to pray in your old way."

"The Three Hermits"
makes clear two cardinal points about prayer.

The first point is this.
There is no one way for everybody to pray.
You will probably find as many ways to pray
as you find people who pray.

The closest Jesus ever came
to giving his followers a "way" to pray
was the Lord's Prayer.
But Jesus intended this prayer
to be illustrative, not restrictive.
St. Augustine says of the Lord's Prayer:

"What we ought to pray for
is in it;
what is not in it,
we ought not to pray for."

"The Three Hermits"
makes clear, also, a second point about prayer.
It is this: Keep your prayer simple.

Whatever complicates prayer
is probably best forgotten.
Father Dan Lord was right when
he gave this advice to a young person:

"Keep your prayer simple.
Talk to God as to a Father,
to Christ as to a brother,
and to the Holy Spirit as a constant companion."

"Prayer in its simplest definition is merely a wish turned Godward."
PHILLIPS BROOKS

Reflection

Imagine you are vacationing alone
in a cabin miles away from all civilization.
It is two in the morning; you cannot sleep.
You get up and walk barefoot out of doors.

You feel the morning dew on the soft grass.
You look up at the clear night sky,
peopled with millions of beautiful, bright stars.
You listen to the voices
of thousands of beetles and crickets
blending in a symphony of night music.

A remarkable feeling of joy and peace
floods into your body and soul.
You stand there, lost in the loveliness
of the night world—God's world.

"O Lord, our Lord,
your greatness is seen in all the world! . . .

"When I look at the sky,
which you have made,
at the moon and the stars,
which you set in their places—
what is man,
that you think of him;
mere man,
that you care for him? . . .

"O Lord, our Lord,
your greatness is seen in all the world!"

PSALM 8

SOURCES

Anderson, George. "Group Praying in Jail." *Review for Religious,* January 1978.

Blanton, Smiley. "The Bible's Timeless—and Timely—Insights." *Reader's Digest,* August 1966.

Cahill, Tim. "Sky Diving: Rapture of the Heights." *Outside,* November/December 1978.

Campion, Nardi Reeder. "Whose God is Dead?" *Reader's Digest,* October 1966.

Carrel, Alexis. *Prayer.* Translated by Ducie de Ste Croix Wright. Morehouse: 1948.

Carrel, Alexis. "Prayer Is Power." *Reader's Digest,* November 1962.

Cassidy, Sheila. "Prayer under Duress." *National Review,* 22 July 1977.

Chesterton, G. K. "The Wise Men." *The Collected Poems of G. K. Chesterton.* New York: Dodd, Mead & Company, 1951.

Madame Chiang Kai-shek (Meiling, Soong). "The Power of Prayer." *Reader's Digest,* August 1955.

Day, Dorothy. *House of Hospitality.* New York: Harper & Row, 1963.

de Mello, Anthony. *Sadhana: A Way to God.* Gujarat, India: Anand Press.

Durkin, Jim. "Living the Word." *New Covenant.* November, 1979.

Eareckson, Joni and Musser, Joe. *Joni.* Grand Rapids, Michigan: Zondervan, 1976.

Frank, Anne. *Anne Frank: The Diary of a Young Girl.* New York: Doubleday, 1952.

Godfrey, Arthur. "The Fire or the Scrap Heap?" *The Guideposts Treasury of Faith.* New York: Doubleday 1970.

Happold, F. C. *Prayer and Meditation*. Pelican.

Ipswitch, Elaine. *Scott Was Here*. New York: Delacorte, 1979.

Johnston, William. *Silent Music: The Science of Meditation*. New York: Harper & Row, 1974.

Kennedy, Joseph A. *Relax and Live*. Prentice-Hall, 1953.

Kierkegaard, Soren. *The Journals of Kierkegaard*. Translated, edited, and with an introduction by Alexander Dru. New York: Harper & Brothers, 1958. Entry of January 6, 1839. Adapted.

Lagemann, John Kord. "To Know Yourself, Meditate." *Together,* Ann Arbor, Michigan: United Methodist Publishing House, October 1960.

Lapierre, Michael. "Progress in Prayer." *The Way,* July 1970.

Maloney, George. *Stages of Contemplation*. National Catholic Reporter cassette. National Catholic Reporter Publishing Company.

Melville, Herman. *Moby Dick; or, The White Whale*. Standard edition. New York: Russell & Russell, 1963.

Merton, Thomas. *Seeds of Contemplation*. "Mental Prayer." Westport, Connecticut: Greenwood, 1979 (reprint of 1949 edition).

Miller, Keith. *The Taste of New Wine*. Word Books, 1965.

Mills, Joan. "You Belong to Me." *Reader's Digest,* June 1977.

Padovano, Anthony. *Belief in Human Life*. New York: Paulist Press.

Perera, Eva Lewis. "Reading Aloud: A Vanishing Commodity of Culture." *Christianity Today,* 8 June 1979.

Salinger, J. D. "Teddy." From *Nine Stories.* New York: Little, Brown & Company, 1953.

Salter, James. "Getting High." *Life,* August 1979.

Summers, Dwayne. *The Upper Room,* November-December 1978.

Szathmary, Louis. *The Chef's Secret Cook Book.* New York: Quadrangle/New York Times Book Company, 1972.

Thomas, Piri. *Down These Mean Streets.* New York: Alfred Knopf and Company, 1967.

Van Breeman, Peter. *As Bread That Is Broken.* Denville, New Jersey: Dimension Books.

von Meysenbug, Malwida. *Memoiren Einer Idealistin.* 5te Auflage, 1900, iii, 166.

Walsh, Mary Ann. "Unbelievable Intimacy." *Sign* Magazine, October 1979.

Williams, Tennessee. *The Night of the Iguana.* From *The Theater of Tennessee Williams,* Vol. 4. New York: New Directions, 1972.

ACKNOWLEDGEMENTS *Continued from page ii*

Smiley Blanton, "The Bible's Timeless—and Timely—Insights," in *Reader's Digest,* August 1966. Reprinted by permission.

Tim Cahill, "Sky Diving: Rapture of the Heights," in *Outside,* November/December 1978. Reprinted by permission.

Narid Reeder Campion, "Whose God Is Dead?" in *Reader's Digest,* October 1966. Reprinted by permission.

Alexis Carrel, "Prayer is Power," in *Reader's Digest,* November 1962. Reprinted by permission.

Dr. Shelia Cassidy, "Prayer Under Duress," in *National Review,* July 22, 1977. Reprinted by permission.

G. K. Chesterton, "The Wise Men," in The Collected Poems of G. K. Chesterton. Dodd, Mead & Co., 1951. Reprinted by permission.

Jim Durkin, *Living the Word.* Copyright © 1979 by Jim Durkin. Reprinted by permission of Servan Publications, Box 8617, Ann Arbor, Michigan 48107.

Anne Frank, *Anne Frank: The Diary of a Young Girl.* Copyright © 1952 by Otto H. Frank. Reprinted by permission of Doubleday & Co., Inc. in the United States and by Vallentine, Mitchell & Co. in the United Kingdom.

Arthur Godfrey, "The Fire or the Scrap Heap," which appeared in *The Guideposts Treasury of Faith* by Guideposts Associates. Copyright © 1970 by Guideposts Associates, Inc. Reprinted by permission of Doubleday & Co., Inc.

Joseph A. Kennedy, *Relax and Live,* Prentice-Hall, Inc. Copyright © 1953 by Joseph A. Kennedy. Reprinted by permission of Prentice-Hall, Inc., Englewood Cliffs, New Jersey 07632.

John Kord Lagemann, "To Know Yourself, Meditate," in *Reader's Digest,* December 1960. Reprinted by permission.

Michael Lapierre, "Progress in Prayer," in *The Way,* July 1970. Reprinted by permission.

Anthony de Mello, S.J. *Sadhana: A Way to God.* Reprinted by permission.

Joan Mills, "You Belong to Me," in *Reader's Digest,* June 1977. Reprinted by permission.

Eva Lewis Perera, "Reading Aloud: A Vanishing Commodity of Culture," in *Christianity Today,* June 8, 1979. Copyright by *Christianity Today.* Reprinted by permission of *Christianity Today.*

James Salter, "Getting High," in *Life,* August 1979. Reprinted by permission.

The Breakaway Program includes four components that can be used individually or in any combination.

The Breakaway Book
The book divides into 28 steps. Each step includes an Instruction and Reflection section.

Twenty-Eight Handout Sheets
Featuring stories, activities, and week-by-week journals. The Handout Sheets are available in two forms: Blackline Master Kit or Ready-to-Use Booklets (packs of 12 only).

Two Cassettes
Mark Link narrates the 28 reflections of the book with music and sound effects.

Presenter's Guide
Practical ideas and instructions for implementing the Breakaway Program with groups or on a one-to-one basis.

For information write to:

Argus Communications
Dept. 50
One DLM Park
Allen, Texas 75002